LOTERIA

A POETRY COLLECTION

Esteban Miranda

Loteria
© 2025, Esteban Miranda
ISBN: 978-1-966337-07-2

Library of Congress control number: 202590995

First Edition, 2025

Printed in the United States of America

Edited by: Esteban Miranda
Cover Design by: Emmanuel Enciso
Layout Design by: Emmanuel Enciso

Dedication

To my family and loved ones. My brother, who left this world early, but your name and person is not forgotten. Octavio, enjoy this book.

Dedicatoria

A mi familia y seres queridos. Mi hermano, que partió prematuramente, pero tu nombre y tu persona no se olvidan. Octavio, disfruta de este libro.

Acknowledgments

To my family — the heart and soul of my journey. To my parents, who taught me the value of hard work, being true, and family. Your sacrifices and strength to come to this country for a better life and the journey you took to figure it out helped pave the way for everything I am and strive to be, true resilience. To my sister and brother (look at me, look at this book, look at this book), my girlfriend, my forever partners in laughter and chaos. Thank you for the memories, the lessons, and the constant support. To my son Marcos, you brighten my life every single day. To my nieces and nephews, whose bright eyes and boundless energy remind me of the beauty in our culture and the importance of passing down our traditions and creating new opportunities for people of color. To my friends, my chosen family, for the shared stories, the countless laughs, and the "support." And to my immediate family — you fill my life with so much love. To my son, you are my proudest legacy. My stepdaughter, you are a beautiful part of my story. Thank you for making my life richer and my heart fuller.

Con todo mi corazón y alma
Esteban Miranda

Table of Contents

LOTERIA

A POETRY COLLECTION

The fuming sound woke me up.
What place was this? Pants down,
blood on my hands,
and my shirt was missing.
Walked around.

That sound again.
Rinsed my mouth
at the foreign sink,
dry saliva
from beer, whiskey,
a fishbowl that was shared,
and cement?

Again, the sound.
A wake-up call
with people
lying on the floor,
unfamiliar.

EL GALLO

The restroom
was a safe place
for self-reflection.
An index finger worth
of toothpaste to brush
the breath of the soon-
to-come hangover.

The half couch i
woke up from
still warm.
Cleaned up
as much as possible.

Waited for the sound again,
it wasn't a crow,
"Get Out."

Too sharp the shine,
too bright the grin,
He dances where the saints begin.
Red suit crisp,
horns held high
the devil's dressed in virtue's tie.

Not sin,
but polish,
turns the tide,
too much pride in being right inside.
He quotes the holy,
walks the line,
halo's glare becomes malign.

No whiskey here,
no smoke, no lies
just ego's flame
in saintly disguise.
He's fast, he prays,
he leads the choir,
But every note played
stokes quite a fire.

EL DIABLITO

The more he's good, the worse he gets,
each virtue sewn
with silken debts.
He loves to judge,
he smiles to scold,
with kindness carved in marbled cold.

El Diablito, dressed so clean,
a mirror polished
much too keen.
He whispers,
"perfect,"
sweet and low
and that's the start of all you owe.

3

She would laugh at the late talks of pussy,
shit,
politics,
and the fucken world.
After a laugh attack,
a long drag
clouded her face,
laughing,
drinking the last of the whiskey,
the smell of vomit,
perfume,
clean clothes.
A tamed lady
that walked out on me,
not the last,
but an unforgotten one.

LA DAMA

4

Nadie se salvará, nadie verá lo mismo.
The person well-dressed likes the shoes,
the suit, the grease on the hair that lets them hide a past,
lets them hide a truth that they knew,
a truth that is better than hidden,
pressed pantalones, gloves, bow-tie, creases on the pants,
a monocle to see another future,
another hope,
another life.

EL CATRIN

They argued at the door of the cab.
Umbrella opening,
closing,
Door slamming.
door opening.

An angered man,
a patient woman,
the man twice her age,
the woman a hopeful age.
She spoke, he barely listened.

The red on his face spread
like spilled milk on the kitchen table.
He held it, knowing his truth.
She, not knowing the truth,
gave the umbrella.

He slammed the door,
laughed at the rain.
The woman's tears ran down slower
than the rain that started hitting her.

EL PARAGUAS

She walked away with heavy tears.
He opened the umbrella to the nearest
woman.
Red-faced, horny, and lonely as the falling
rain drops.

6

She called it her "kitty kat."
She said she kept it tight,
clean,
fresh.

She had been hurt.
She said, "I've
been broken, still am,
sorry."

As she drank
her tea in the water,
she smiled,
her broken English
repeated, "my kitty kat."

The water calmed him
as he just stared.
It would be a kitty kat
that was forever underwater,
forever away from any
breath.

LA SIRENA

7

Una persona
gripped it and knew
nothing about anything.
They just knew how to be honest,
hard,
and that's what brought
a wanting citizen,
the one born in the land,
a student.
The other one that are willing to learn from all:
a banker, drove what the rest could not;
a cop, the barely invited;
a teacher, that helped keep it together.
All of the climb, support to the end,
the final step, fin de uno.

LA ESCALERA

The botella de vida.
It did not rest on the table.
The liquid was strong
and never easy to keep down.
I drank from it
most of the time.
The shape changed
with the days.
It spoke truths,
lied at times
more than a kid at recess.
But it brought the most laughs,
tears, and bravery
than any other person alive.
It opened truths of forgotten
memories,
truths that no one heard but me.

LA BOTELLA

9

Aquí me tienes, medio tapado,
no por miedo, por lo callado.
Un barril viejo, madera y clavo,
guarda más que pulque bravo.

Me metí solo, por no mirar,
las horas muerden, no saben parar.
No fue castigo, ni fue destierro,
fue pausa mía
un encierro tierno.

Porque allá afuera todo es prisa,
chisme, trabajo, promesa lisa.
Aquí adentro el tiempo cede,
y hasta el alma, mira, se me queda.

Oyes el mundo, yo oigo el eco,
de mi pensar, de un sueño seco.
"¿Dónde estás?" gritan con celo.
"En mi barril… hablando al cielo."

EL BARRIL

Salgo nomás cuando ya es justo,
cuando el reloj me hable con gusto.
Hasta entonces, déjenme aquí,
con el silencio y un poco de mi.

10

It grew.
It grew up and sideways,
up, left, down, right,
drifted with the breeze
leaned with the storms,
shed when the timing
wasn't right.
It kept its growth,
nothing made it leave.

EL ARBOL

I forgot it on the roof of the car.
Bagged and all.
Sweetness that would never be tasted,
eaten.
A melon that slid,
fell,
and became
the ground.

Seeds that would not
be planted, sprouted
and tasted again.

EL MELÓN

12

¿Qué es ser valiente?
¿Hacer el trabajo del día?
¿Hacer trabajo de la noche?
El valiente doesn't care
about the opinions of the lands.
Travels for work and takes it,
claims it and makes it work,
tames the lands where footprints
are left.

EL VALIENTE

13

A hat people wear, I've seen slanted at the rim,
a slight curve from the drunken falls.
A teased frame from the miles it was dragged,
the morboso head it rested on.
Only providing inches of shade,
covering dañado thoughts... that's all that was needed,
the hats people wear,
their heads,
they are never shown.

EL GORRITO

14

Always, Never, late,
an appointment that gets the worst part of it.
A lonely task that is often confused,
"I want una vida,"
"no la tuya,"
to share a moment together
before the end,
to share a moment
that can be remembered.
"No Puedo tocar,"
Life
"puedo tocar"
Death.

LA MUERTE

I sat and ordered my second drink before happy hour ended.
Saved two dollars,
saved breaking a twenty.
A beer to sip,
but a shot of whiskey
to be alive.
The young and eager bartender
serving drinks to the new people
walking in, wanting to know
their stories.

Watched the bar TVs switch from the afternoon
fútbol to the evening football.
I got to see the real show,
behind the bar,
hopeful but all a piece of work.
I laughed at the men trying to get laid,
"I would take care of you,"
"You don't belong behind the bar, you are a trophy."

LA PERA

I was there early enough to see
that she was still attached to the earth.
Attached that the happy hour words were ignored.
Enjoyed
but ignored.

She carried a flag everywhere she went.
She couldn't walk or talk without it.
It was a goal,
the colors–blue, white, red, with a peace
sign where the stars should have been.
She loved the world.
She was free from loving someone.
She was free from the world.
She held it with blistering palms,
an extension of her thoughts.

LA BANDERA

17

I listened to the bandolon player talk about music like no one understood it.

"They didn't understand the music."

The time had changed feeling into a fast food of processed studio of sounds.

He played for the moment and didn't want it to be captured, played with barely a dream, but a time and place to be forgotten from the rest of the world.

EL BANDOLON

I gave up on yesterday,
a time where it would have
made sense,
would have made me think
he gave himself to an empty sidewalk,
drunk me,
wasted,
trying to get rid
of a hangover,

just two shadows
stool and notes

leaning on earth

trying to catch
a breath for today.

EL VIOLENCELLO

19

He crawled, mumbled words he had spoken to others
other women,
very few men,
and occasionally street dogs that he claimed as pets
half passed out,
looking for a place that was only familiar to him,
the streets and alleys,
the starts of the strays wandering the gated,
chained-fenced houses.
Knock knock.

The light came on,
the curtain swayed,
he knocked again.
The door opened,
closed, she stood looking,
over him as he swayed.
She stood tall, her last time,
she kissed his forgotten head,
went inside.
Smiled back at him from the window.
She closed the door for the first and last time.

LA GARZA

El pajaro could not fly, it hid in the dirt,
peach fuzz,
cerebral palsy arms,
legs still strong and able to walk to the trees.
It ate the insects that were not fast enough to escape.

come,
come,
comiendo,

The bird did not chirp,
it just knew how to walk and eat.
A fallen bird that could not fly,
but found new wings

EL PAJARO

21

She pulled her kids.
She held their hands,
walked them, ready for school,
bathed, fed, and groomed.

Took the long walk back,
picked up cans and bottles,
planned their futures
with every few cents
she collected.

Her hands didn't stop.
No gloves,
gentle but callused hands
that felt a need to do.

La Mano

It was the night she had enough.
I laughed, smiled, and drank
with her.
She wore them,
the fucken boots
that made her stand
at the bar
instead of sitting.

She looked more like a woman
in them.
Every word heard,
her steps echoed her
thoughts.
It was the last
time her boots
walked the sticky floor of that bar,
she knew,
he knew that those boots
were meant to be heard.

LA BOTA

23

She laughed at the moon,
"It's never the same,
the nights change it."
She was right,
nights change.

I looked away
and faced la Luna.
She reflected tomorrow's light
and I smiled.

LA LUNA

"If they don't look like me then no,"
squawk,
"How can I walk around my neighborhood now,"
squawk,
"What colors do you have?
They don't look like us, we have to work harder,"
squawk,
"We welcome it, but it hasn't been right,"
squawk.

"My color matters,"
squawk.
"Why am I always to be blamed?
they are coming after us."
squawk,
"We have to protect ourselves
keep to ourselves, that's the only way,"
gawk.
"Let them argue about land that isn't theirs."

The parrot repeats what has been spoken,
but doesn't take flight.
Just squawk.

EL COTORRO

25

An empty glass,
yes, the shot was gone,
but another would follow.

Mornings,
afternoons,
nights
blurred
like the condensation
from the lingering alcohol.

What does a drunk do?
Breathes with the drink,
the drunk doesn't know.
It is, still a drunk.

EL BORRACHO

26

a stone
was used to make flavor
bring spice
blend
grind
mix

combine
what
is expected
what is tolerated

used
for the moment
and never kept
the same

changed
every time
never kept the shape

EL MOLCAJETE

a stone
that was never
fully used.

27

No más hay uno, y qué capricho,
Quedate solo, sin su gemelo.
No hay repuesto, ni hay desquicio
que nos regale un paralelo.

Este tambor de carne y ruido,
carga amor, coraje, y olvido.
Le das y le das, y él sigue fiel,
aunque le quiebren su papel.

No hay copia, no hay segundo intento,
ni garantía ni salvamiento.
Te toca usar el que trajiste,
con todo el miedo que escondiste.

Y duele más por ser tan único,
por ser de todos el más inútil
cuando lo rompes sin querer
cuando lo usaste para huir.

EL CORAZON

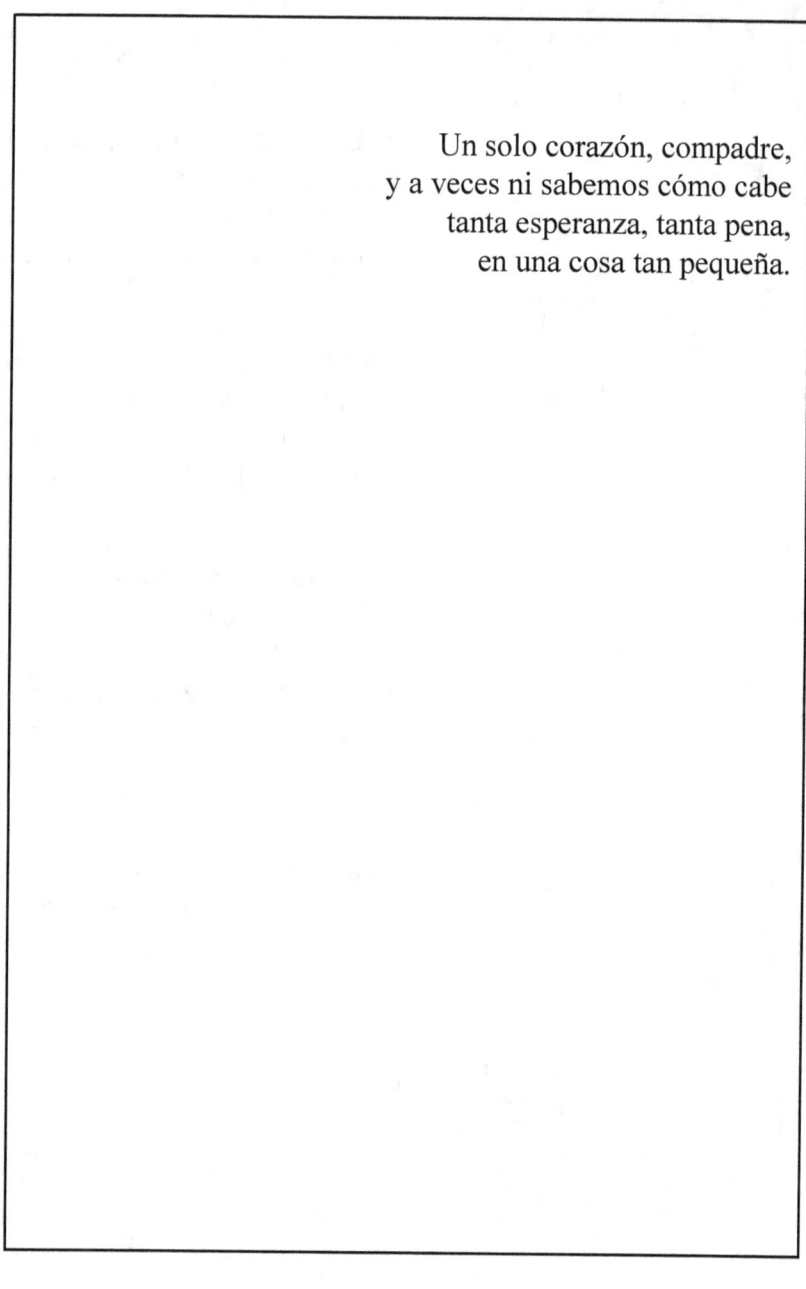

Un solo corazón, compadre,
y a veces ni sabemos cómo cabe
tanta esperanza, tanta pena,
en una cosa tan pequeña.

Seedless or seed,
the taste is the same
sticky,
soft crunch.
One brings back
the same fruit.
The other lets it be.

Which one tastes better?
The one and done?
Or the repeated?

LA SANDÍA

29

a turn of the wrist
a flick of a hand
the sweat of the bujes
a position of the snares
Graze of a symbol
Graze of a symbol
Graze of a symbol
A smile of the snare.
A feel for the night.
Steady
ready
roving
growing.

EL TAMBOR

Tomato juice, splashes of hot sauce, two shots of vodka.
a drink of the fooled
a celery stick that out-yellows a ripe banana,
a lime to hide the flavor of the previous night,
a crustacean
hanging
drinking
wasted.

EL CAMARÓN

31

I took aim.
Stared.
Smiled.
Walked up.
No idea on what I wanted to do.
Say.
Think.

I laughed,
said, "Hi."
She said "Hey,"
with a smirk.
Laughed again.
She smiled,
grabbed my hand,
and took me
to dance.

She laughed.
We laughed.
She stared.
We stared.
She leaned in.

LAS JARAS

I leaned in closer.
Smelled the last
shot,
sweat,
beauty.

"I aimed for you,
only, you."
She smiled.
We smiled.
"Bullseye,"

she said.

32

Toquen la canción de amor,
la canción que hace el tiempo parar
ninguna persona puede hablar.

La canción que se llevo la noche.
La toco el músico,
todo las personas mirando,
pero ningunas escuchando
su ultimas notas.

El Músico

Las piernas de su cuerpo.
No pueden tocar todo.
Un momento sin peligro,
sin un segundo de tímido,
sin palabras dichas,
sin mente,
solo alma,
solo fe,
la telarañas de la noche,
los ojos que miran
las reflexiones del cielo.

La Araña

34

Trying to make sense,
but how much sense?
Enough to follow?
Enough to know the truth?
Enough to leave?
Enough to live out
a life I haven't lived?

EL SOLDADO

Not all stars dazzle, not all stars burn,
Some whisper light, the world won't learn.
They pulse in shadows, pale and small,
A quiet heartbeat in the sprawl.

No wishing on them, no grand design,
No sailors led by their gentle shine.
They flicker faint on the cosmic seam,
The ones that hover between seen and dream.

They don't command, they don't declare,
Their glimmer hums in thinner air.
Forgotten sparks in a shouting sky,
Not every star is meant to fly.

But still they shine, though dim, though weak,
A light for those who dare to seek.
For even a whisper in endless night
Is a promise made a soft, quiet light.

LA ESTRELLA

36

After the last drink,
I went to eat.
Drunk me
lost the keys,
phone,
and laptop
that served
as a table.
Boiled water.
Top Ramen,
broke some off,
ate it like chips,
emptied the packets
into the pot.

Tossed the noodles
because they burned,
the night's water
escaped them.
No ramen,
no food,
just another stain
on the kitchen floor.

EL CAZO

What is a world?
The world that is shared.
The world that is torn.
The world that is fought?
The world that is not thought
as a whole but an individual thought?

A world that has lasted.
A world that has not backed down,
time that does not end.
A world that does not stop
its motion, harvests, and contains.

A person, a group, a movement
decides its end.
Decides it, ends with them.
No.
El mundo va a vivir.
Nosotros no.

EL MUNDO

38

Last of his kind,
a shadow on the red horizon,
footsteps quiet as forgotten drums.

He speaks to winds that know his name,
to trees that lean in memory.
Every breath, a prayer, a curse, a claim
an echo of the unreturned.

Bones like flint, eyes like the edge of a blade,
sharp with a past that no longer answers.

The stars watch him,
the rivers whisper his own forgotten tongue,
and he moves through the dusk,
unfollowed,
unforgotten.

EL APACHE

Walked into interviews,
gave them 15 minutes of my best words:
Hard-working
Loyal
Long-term
Leader
Team player
They said yes.

They said yes.
Yes!
What's the work environment?
"We want different points of views.
We want diversity.
We want culture."

They said yes,
I said no.

EL NOPAL

40

Struck with boredom,
no tengo nada,
but I know where we can
find money.
A young kid with his parent's
change.
The thought of spending
the last hours eating street food,
investing in arcades, and bottles
of pure-sugar Coke.

The bottom part of the luggage
hidden from sunlight, dirt of the land,
hands of a child.

The small creature,
wild and eager to protect itself,
stung the native because of the chance
of fun.

I left the next day,
not knowing where

EL ALACRAN

he had been stung,
whether he died.
He searched
for the money first.
Was it his fault,
had he not seen money?
Or was it mine?

41

No me cortes, no me tomes,
déjame ser un misterio en el aire.
Mi espina es filo, mi pétalo suerte,
mi perfume un pacto que huele a muerte.

Déjame en rama, en sombra y viento,
en la distancia del pensamiento.
No todo amor se debe tener,
no todo deseo se debe saber.

Hay verdades que sangran lento,
que pierden luz al primer intento.
¿No ves? Mi belleza es de lejos,
un suspiro rojo en tus reflejos.

Déjame ser lo que nunca se alcanza,
la rosa intacta, la eterna danza.

LA ROSA

Bone and hollow, a watcher still,
eyes that never close, never fill.
Death that lingers, white and bare,
breathless, timeless, always there.

It sees the streets, the rise and fall,
the laughter, the cries, the whispers small.
It leans on graves, it haunts the light,
a patient ghost, a silent rite.

It never claims, just counts the days,
watches the dance, the winding maze.
For every ending feeds its gaze,
a quiet promised life always strays.

For every skull, a life once bright,
a heartbeat cast into endless night.
But even bones can dream of grace,
of finding peace, of finding place.

La Calavera

43

I rang the campana every day I left–
when I would go to work,
to the gym,
to walk the dog that loved–
it rang for years
until it broke.
It broke and I could finally
look at my own shadow.

LA CAMPANA

I dropped a truth.
What was expected
to be listened to, digested,
taken was wasted.
A step back from reality
and left behind.
A time of confusion,
for self-reflection,
a moment to bounce back,
grow and to pull together
the fragile pieces that have chipped
away.

EL CANTARITO

45

In the hush of green, the breath of pine,
I shed my crown, my sharpened spine.
Antlers fall like whispered leaves,
a silent gift the forest receives.

I give my armor to the loam,
to feed the roots, to call the home.
Let the fawns take up the trail,
let them breathe where shadows pale.

Every winter strips me bare,
but spring will always find me there,
lighter, quieter, bold and free,
a promise carried by the trees.

In the wild, we lose, we grow,
and every horn must crack, let go.
Life demands the strongest part,
the willing wound, the open heart.

EL VENADO

I laughed at the help.
Fuck them.
Fuck help.
Fuck
being normal.
Words
and actions
that hurt and were said
every one of those people
slept,
tried to,
and woke
up again
to do it again.

EL SOL

47

A crown is not jewelry, a hat,
an image of a figure.
It's a pen with paper.
It's the hand that holds it,
a mind that writes the future.
It's the drinks it took
to express unspoken words.
It's the truth where there's none.

La corona no tiene ningún pensamiento,
only truth, the truth that has been forgotten
and praised by few.

LA CORONA

Soy remo y río,
soy viento y piel,
la fuerza callada que corta el cieno,
que rompe olas, que sueña en vuelo.

No temo al agua, ni al cielo gris,
ni al canto sordo del mal decir.
Soy mujer y corriente, sin miedo al abismo,
mi canto es firme, mi paso es ritmo.

Que me miren de lejos, que murmuren bajo,
que piensen que es locura el ir sin atajo.
No saben que el silencio es mi mapa,
que la luna me guía, que el eco me llama.

La chalupa solitaria no se hunde, no se calla,
se alza, se lanza, y nunca se talla.
Porque en cada remo llevo la historia,
de mil mujeres que buscan su gloria.

LA CHALUPA

49

El olor.
El olor de la noche.
El olor de el tiempo.
El polar de las personas.
El tiempo en que no recuerda,
pero afirma que no pude oler,
los que saben oler.

EL PINO

50

It was the salmon.
It took it to the next level,
a taste,
a smell
that was pure.

The river
that cleaned
guts and steps
of creatures,
it flowed.

The salmon swam,
kept going,
didn't stop
for the one salmon.

EL PESCADO

51

I stood,
slanted,
leaning,
swaying to the wind.
The sky clear,
paradise California sun,
with the day breeze
caressing the leaves.

The shade creating
enough for butterflies.
The roots still inching
to spread,
to be able to see more.
To be able to stand taller
than the butterfly.

LA PALMA

I left it.
Left it in the shaded area
where the sun can sometimes expose it,
where the morning sprinkler can wet the soil,
where a child's hand can't fuck with it.
The hummingbird sage.
A place where nothing
but growth stays
resting,
waiting,
opening to shriveled leaves,
growing stems
to fit in.
I left it
there,
protected,
protected from you,
protected from me.

La Maceta

53

Strings like whispers, breath like wine,
I lose my way in the curves of a line.
Fingers wander, pulse, and sigh
a ghost in the wood, a note in the sky.

I'm pulled by echoes, by threads of sound,
by the trembling air, by the ache unbound.
Every chord a ripple, every pluck a tear,
a gentle chaos, a breath made clear.

Lost in the hum, in the shiver, the break,
in the sweet, sharp ache of a heart half-awake.
The muse pulls tight, my will unwinds,
And I am but a vessel for forgotten minds.

So let me drift, let me stray,
For every lost note, has its day.
Every dissonance finds its part,
every stray string sings to the heart.

EL ARPA

He went after what he liked,
the clean,
the cute,
the clever,

the people that came out at night
but make it annoying,

annoying to be out,
and that it will last
the entire night.

He didn't know them.
Just walked, talked,
and traveled with them.
Sulking the night.

Annoyed that they didn't
walk as fast,
talk with the ideas of today,
and that they wanted to stay
at one place,
one pond.
He saw the poisonings of the night.

LA RANA

LOTERIA!!!

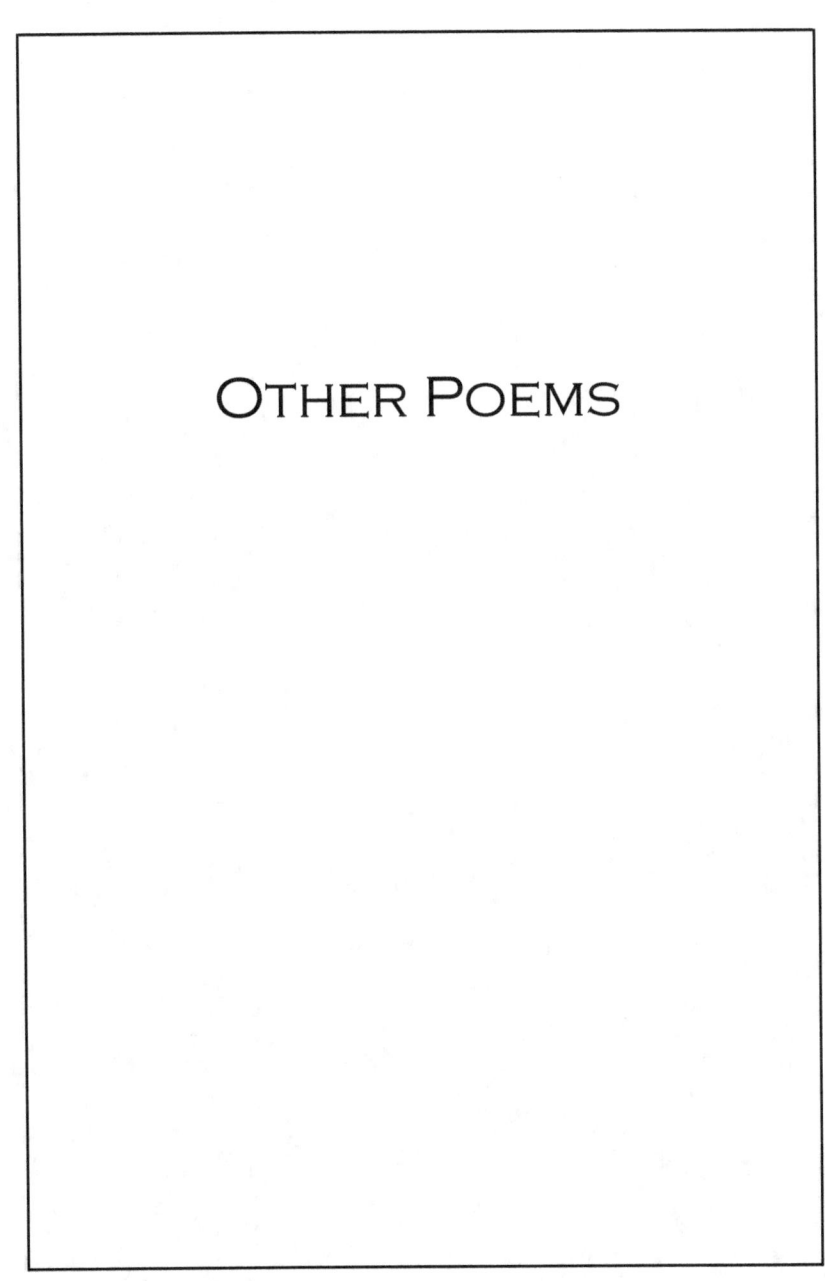

OTHER POEMS

Shared the last seven minutes with a beautiful
woman. meaningless conversation.
my saliva in her mouth. her
lipstick on my teeth. the
usual seven minutes
reduced to three.
will it change
after or will
it be the
same as
it gets
to the
butt.

SEVEN MINUTES

"Body aching."
Updated online.
Thousands of dollars to reduce
years of age. Doc
said recovery would hurt.
Take pills once every four hours.
Hope to be younger, but
No use hiding old prune hands
behind the keyboard.

"Bed rest."
Updated online.
I get to be on
my laptop.
Windows 95 running smooth,
imagine anything better? No.
Pills taken like tic
tac swallowing teens
out on the first date
nervous and waiting
for their first kiss.

...UPDATING

"Serenity sinking in." Updated.
Five likes.
Eyes closing
No more pain.

Walking into an abandoned house
trying to find some peace.
They should usually be quiet, lonely, and dirty.
Rats bigger than footballs,
spiders that make your house ones look childish,
termites you can hear eating through the structure
of the leftover home.
Nothing sounds louder when you're trying to be quiet.
Why try to be silent in an abandoned house?

Creep into a room with a child's bed fully made.
Did they forget to take some furniture?
A child's bedroom with handprints on the walls
that used to have some color to them,
bed frame and drawers dusty,
size 11K shoes, sandals, and slippers
nicely tucked under some clothes in the closet.

Looking at the door frame
with measurements and dates
engraved to the house.

MEASUREMENTS

3'5" – 11/30/10
3'8" – 5/12/11
4'0" – 10/29/11
and nothing else.
The quieter the house,
the louder the walls.

Hello,
Why are you late?
I'm actually running on time.
Hello.
Hello.
Hello,
I only have a $5, can I get a courtesy ride?
Hello,
Only have 35 cents.
Hello,
You're late.
Hello.
Hello.
Hello.
Hello,
Do you go to the blue line station?
Hello,
Don't talk to me I'm on my phone'.
Hello.
Hello.
Hello.
Hello,
Hi,

ROUTE 130 HELLO'S

Hello, how are you?
I'm good, you?
I'm fine, thanks.

Empty glasses with perspiration
on the outside and three drops
of the cheapest beer from the local
applebee's fills Tuesday night's loneliness.

Never been able to make the drink
specials but always in time to catch
the bus boy grab a handful
of the waitress's ass
and her smile back with reassurance.

My thought is that she might be using
him because the bartender took
his fifteen minutes right with her
and rushed outside as she made her way
into her car.

These people fuck each other
each time they have the same shift,
who fucks them when they don't?

A TUESDAY

An impression that i get when i meet a woman
when words and thoughts are the two
features that stand out.
takes fifteen minutes
for the fluid, shy, and unseen life
to pierce through. it hurts not to say
anything. it hurts not to say the romantic
words that will take away reality.

Why go the path that many broken
lives follow? a date - second date -
- pause for reflection - third date -
- dating – sex - pause again for reflection -
- couple shit – marriage - animosity -
- divorce – ruminate - broken sex -
- forever separate.

I say skip that. let the fervor
stand alone. let the play never end.
let the era be impeccable.
let space be timeless.

let's just go…

AN IMPRESSION THAT I GET

Car crash on the highway as I drove to work,
  news reported man was on the run from the government
  hacked their system all because he wanted to be
  remembered.
At work skyscraping towers of paper to file,
as I work a woman outside cliff jumps off a building
  only to have her chute malfunction and her body splatter
  like a dropped water balloon.
Restroom break and I sit on the toilet seat
reading the engraved graffiti in the stall
 'life is bigger than you, it isn't anything to possess,
        its something you take part in.'
Profound, the graffiti glued to my mind as I went to lunch
  in my car. How can words so true be written by
    someone who writes on restroom walls?
        my cars' brakes fail me as I drive head on to a fuel
truck through the intersection.
E-brake, they never fail, I pull up only to swerve to avoid
the impact
    stranded my watch beeping like crazy, heart rate 170 bpm,
drivers knocking

BPM

on my window screaming if I am okay, take off seat belt, watch and
       slide out of my car, 'I'm okay," I yell to the sky with my arms out.

Drop my watch and crush it with my foot, three-hundred dollars feels rough.
I start running with no destination in mind.
Empty my bank account and continue walking.
Must take part in life.

what are
people allowed
to laugh at?

today someone said
that jokes making
fun of people
aren't
okay.

they're
hurtful
and cause
pain.

laughter
is
laughter.

COLLECT 36

and
it
is
pure.
intimate.
freeing.

Seeing the houses now
still with the same
paint, chipped and cracked .
Winterfresh blue
Big red, red
Extra green
Double-mint off white.
Like gum off school desks.

Sidewalk infested with black spots
and every half block a couch rests on a curb.
People's rented yards with trash
some with unfixable cars
resting on bricks that have layers of rust.
Yard overwhelmed with potted plants
that normally don't grow together.

The corner store owner
painting over spray paint.
He always came early on
thursdays to do that.

HEIGHTS

People die here.
Silent or loud.
Good people sometimes
die screaming.
My neighborhood.

i wish i would remember
to set the time
after the power goes out.
the clock flashes
bright red with meaningless
numbers and the one beer
a night diet helps color
the love i once felt.
music has turned into
songs without hope.
the chorus being
sung by one.
ceiling fan on a low
buzzing rotation
becomes a lullabetic tune.
the pipes sending water
tell me it's a little pass
three forty-five.
a neighbor's morning ritual
that adds to the tune
already being played
to the arduous demons.

NIGHT WAKES

a picture of lips,
a picture of nails,
a picture of rings,
of all assorted colors
that reveal that there's nothing.

layers of empty life
with a body that motions
alongside the crowd.

posts that scream, like me
posts that portray no vision
posts of your best angle
with the right amount
cleavage and a smirk
that makes everyones' eyes dilate.

the endless taps of admiration
fill a breached bucket
that will never overflow.

a present to no one.

POST OF VANITY

Sunrises and you are there,
a bud ready to blossom,
Noon hits same as before
Orchids bow from your presence
Moon wanes in the bed you lay
Curvy stem ready to rest

Day after
Day
Day after
Day

Morning comes and you are hard to bare
My entire day with you would not be awesome
Lunch arrives with a whole world to explore
Like trash, i cannot take your essence
The night comes and yet you still want to stay
Hire an exterminator because you are a pest

Throw all the
cans and bottles
To the trash
you always did

RECYCLE

To you now
i do the same
Don't be sad
it's just a process
because
now
I recycle.

Weeks of dirty car.
So I go around driving
looking for a wash.
Morning special ten dollars.
Left wallet, car still dirty.

Man walking dog stops
at my yard and dog takes shit.
Morning and morning
I see him come to my yard
and he never picks up shit.

Woman buying tea.
Orders a tea called blooming.
Cash only, she has
plastic. Leaves. I order, see
her return and hand her tea.

Does the universe
know that stars and people die?
Scars are left behind,
never to be healed, just felt.
Have you ever left a scar?

SCARS

Tonight we will begin to change some minds.
The sound of sweat will count for some but not
all feel the pain of grass. A trophy finds
a team that fears no one. Destroy the lot.

What more can hands neglect, abuse, declare
and still be true? The scars, the bruises hurt
but any athlete would do it with a glare.
Gripping the bottles waiting for water to squirt.

Though time goes wild inside the game. Obey
the rules and age will not change you. Within
periods people will rejoice the birthday.
When time runs out how do you know you win?
Those fifteen minutes bend and last some more.
Glory and fame before you hit the floor.

GLORY OF THE
GAME

how much can a person put away? The
zippers open and close to reveal items
compressed together so that the overhead
compartment can still be the first and only
option. With small and big items
the baggage gets heavier.
ever heard of traveling light?

SUITCASE

Traveled the elevator. couldn't
doubt what was to come. Chills,
anxiety, intensity.
Windows showed a part of the city
never seen.
The eyes of a grandiose local
were hypnotized by the beauty.
she would never know
that the view made it
perfect,
the first and second time.
building size didn't matter,
the lighting was dark enough
to feel the shadows on the bed,
to feel the structure of the room,
throbbing winds hit to view
the warmth.

rested well that night
and the tower
still stood tall.

TEN STORIES
HIGH

a land has a chance
for its freedom.
citizens
vote for democracy.
but
there's always
one
true monarch
in the
end.

TRUE

You notice that they can't get too close to certain areas
because of health restrictions to others.

You notice that when the smoker needs to
light up, the health code is the last thing in mind.

You notice that a pack can last a day or two,

You notice a smoker can work with the cigarette
in the month and the fumes not affecting their vision.

You notice that when they leave the house
they always do a pack/lighter check.

You notice when a smoker laughs they
don't cover their mouth because the teeth
they had are no longer yellow, but gone.

You notice wrinkles that are supposed to come in years later.

You notice their words, "I can stop whenever,
I'm just trying to finish this pack and that's it",
are as empty as libraries.

WHEN YOU NOTICE
A SMOKER

You notice the first two drags remind you
of the times you masturbate and how relaxed

you felt.

you ever seen a person missing an eye?
you ever said i love you to a person and meant it?
you ever felt that you're already in love
        with a person but they don't know it?
you ever stepped on shit bare footed?
you ever wake up, sit up, and vomit
        last nights drinks and just leave
                it because it wasn't going anywhere?
you ever been kicked on the ribs for no reason?
you ever found a hair, skin, or any unknown
        object in food only to continue eating?
you ever been in complete awe
        after seeing someone attractive?
you ever tried to be friends with a person
        so hard that it comes off annoying?
you ever ate a snack off the floor not knowing
        how long it had been there for until
                the chewing began and not stopped?
you ever made out with someone and not remember
        it until the next day when someone reminded you?
you ever felt like you can change the world
        but don't know where to start?
well, i have…

YOU EVER?

He woke up.
Walked his dog with shorts on,
a shirt that showed his arms.
Cold, warm weather showed his nipples.
Laughed when no one would,
cried at truths,
smiled through tears,
some truths.

He belonged to them.
He was fine with it,
fine that he belonged to them.
A world,
people.
Most wouldn't understand
the marginalized
No one would live that life.

UNTITLED

Publisher's Note

Daxson publishing was created to help marginalized artists publish their work, so the world can hear their voice. The vision for this publishing house is to help people get their work out there, and not have them struggle finding their way through the publishing process. Everyone's voice deserves to be heard, and we are here to help. If you are interested in submitting a manuscript, email daxsonpublishing@gmail.com. Support our cause! Buy our books at daxsonpublishing.com.

www.ingramcontent.com/pod-product-compliance
Lightning Source LLC
Chambersburg PA
CBHW051002140626
46546CB00017B/2440